The Things That Shape You

Amber Hernandez

BookLeaf Publishing

Presentation by *BookLeaf Publishing*

Web: www.bookleafpub.com

E-mail: info@bookleafpub.com

ISBN: 9789358369373

First edition 2023

DEDICATION

This book is dedicated to my parents, Oscar and
Patricia Hernandez.

If I Fall

I can see the other side
But I need to jump.
Am I brave enough to try?
How else will I reach it?

The gap is wide.
Do I have the strength to make it?
If I fall,
How deep is the pit?

If I fall,
Will I find others in that darkness?
Will anyone be willing to catch me
Before the worst damage is done?

If I fall,
Can I get back out?

I'm Unsure

I'm unsure of how to proceed
With a particular situation
That I find myself in.
How many people should I
Open up to?
How many people would
Have helpful advice for me?
If I follow it, will I regret it?
Or will I be glad
That I asked for their input?
I don't know . . .
I don't know.
I prefer to keep things private,
So it feels uncomfortable
To open up to others
And have them weigh in
On my life.
I also don't want
To ask too many people about it
Because if they have conflicting advice
And I only listen to one,
Would the others think
I don't trust them as much?
Would they take it personally?
Would it be harder for me

To decide what to do
If I learned of more options
Available to me?
I don't know . . .
I don't know.

Ocean Waves

There is something about
The ocean that terrifies me,
And I feel it in my limbs
When I walk into it.

It is so incredibly large
While I am still yet so small.
I can only stand in the shallow parts
Because it can knock me down so easily.

If I lose the ability to stand,
I am at the mercy of waves
That progressively get stronger
And answer to no one on the beach.

The ocean is not a friendly place
For someone who likes to
Feel in control.
It is anxiety-inducing.

When you look out into the water
Looking for a friend
To make sure they are okay
And the waves hide them from you?

It's the stuff of nightmares
To think for a moment
What would I do without them?
Please, show me they are safe.

And the wave comes down,
And you see them smiling
And having fun
And you can breathe again.

Fur

I was so nervous about picking you up that day.
You were too small to know what was
happening,
But you were getting a new home.

You were probably too small to even think
The one you were in was yours,
Even for a moment.

But I took you,
And you didn't mind.
Then you became mine.

And I had to learn how to care for you
And give you a schedule and structure
When I wasn't good at having those for myself.

But I learned with you
And you learned because of me,
Though we still have more to go.

You used to bite me
When I tried to pet you,
Since you were teething.

Now you roll over
And expose your furry underside
To demand belly rubs.

And your little leg kicks
And your eyes close
And you try to lick my hand in thanks.

I asked for you
And I got you,
So I should care for you.

And I do.
Even though I can't leave the house
Without being covered in your fur.

When I Was Sixteen

When I was sixteen,
I was followed by a car full of young men.
I almost didn't hear the low rumbling of the
engine,
Close behind me.

I turned around,
And they sped away, laughing.
But what if I hadn't?
Would I be here today?

I never wanted to walk alone again
After that day.
My sense of safety was gone.
I was shaken.

I was only looked at
And I felt violated,
Though I was fully clothed.
Why should it be that way?

Don't I have a right to walk on the same soil we
were both born in?
Aren't I as human and capable as you?
Why should I live looking over my shoulder,

While you live in my lifetime?

Don't you know your eyes are venom?
They sting my memories.
They burn my sense of freedom
And affect me for the rest of my life.

And you,
You go on as if nothing happened.

Lisp

When I was a kid,
I had a lisp.
And I didn't think much of it
Until another kid told me
That I talked like a snake.
And I said it wasn't true,
But I knew it was.

I already wouldn't speak much,
But I wanted to speak even less
Because suddenly I was aware
That there was something
Wrong with me.
And sometimes I was asked
To say words that were
Hard for me,
So others could hear
And laugh in my face.

Sometimes I said "no"
To the requests,
But I would be asked
Until I complied.
So I would open my mouth,
Knowing what was coming,

Wanting to get it over with.

I remember thinking,
If I learned sign language
No one would laugh
At the way I would speak
Because they would never
Hear me.

I'm Sorry I'm Quiet

I know I am quiet.
Everybody says so.
It's a practice that is hard to break.

Even with my lack of speech
I've said things I regret,
And those stop me from saying things I won't.

I hate making mistakes
So I try to remove my ability to fail,
But that should not be the answer.

Even so, I am afraid of the things I will say
Because when I say them,
They stay in my memories, haunting me.

How could I say that?
I try to think before I speak,
Yet things slip through the cracks anyway.

I need to be coaxed into sharing my thoughts,
And sometimes I feel so happy that they matter
To others.

However, my lack of experience causes me

To miss the mark when I should have known
what to reply
Because it would be the obvious response to
someone who talks.

I'm sorry I don't know how to talk to you,
But I am trying.
I want to.

Listener

I'm a great listener.
You can ask others
And they'll agree,
I can listen.

It's easy to listen.
You don't have to do anything
But give a bit of your
Attention away, and care.

I don't mind listening to others,
But sometimes I want the same.
It doesn't seem to come as easy
To other people.

I suppose part of my problem is
That I don't want just anyone listening.
I want certain people,
But I don't want to bother them.

They don't really ask
If I need to be listened to,
But that's probably because I haven't
Shown them I need that sometimes.

So instead, I wait until
I'm alone in my room,
And I think and listen to myself
Until I cry.

And sometimes it's not enough,
And I write and listen
To the mess in my head
Getting organized.

Then the clarity is enough
To send me over the edge,
And again,
I cry.

So sometimes,
I draw myself
Feeling my emotions
Openly.

And I feel some relief,
As if I actually did it.
As if I expressed myself
Fiercely.

And again,
I listen to myself.

We Don't Talk Much Anymore

I know we don't talk much anymore.
Part of the reason
Is because I'm not great
At keeping in touch.

But I still care about you
Even though I only see
The things you post
On social media.

We used to hang out
So, so much.
I still have pictures
Of us being silly.

We're adults now,
And we talk differently
To each other
When we do.

And I can tell
We've both been through things
And been shaped
By the experiences we've had.

But no matter
How differently we
Phrase our sentences now,
You were and are still my friend.

Despite the struggle to reach out,
I hope you know
That I always wish you the best
And I am proud of your accomplishments.

Let Me Think For Myself

You don't need to worry about me so much,
I'm going to be okay.
You taught me well enough,
I think I can find my way.

I'm going to make some mistakes,
But that doesn't have to be so bad.
For both of our sakes,
Letting go shouldn't be sad.

We did it!
I might need you sometimes,
But we got through the hard bit.
Please, don't read between the lines.

I'm not trying to push you away,
But let me make decisions in my own life.
Just accept that I should have a say
And I won't purposefully choose strife.

I can think for myself,
You've seen me learn how.
I'll call you when I need your help,
But let me take the reins now.

I've got a great head on my shoulders,
You'll notice when you let me use it.

Can You See the Imprint?

Thank you for being there for me.
You've been such a great example.
I know you doubt your success,
But you're amazing.

Every time I need someone,
I know you're there.
Perhaps you love me too much sometimes,
But that is expected because of who you are.

You've been a second mother,
A counselor and mentor,
Well of inspiration,
And bottomless, protective, fierce love.

Who can stand against an older sister
Who fears no one when defending the younger?
Who gives sacrificially from the fruits of her
hard labor?
Who helped shape from the beginning?

She has as much a claim on any accomplishment
That I can acquire.
Can you see the imprint of her hand
On the back of my shoulder?

Malachi

What would you be like
If you were still here,
Growing and learning
And letting us love you?

How cute would you be?
What would you find interesting?
Would you laugh at my jokes
And find me entertaining?

Would you smile at me
The way you did
When you were just learning
To move those little muscles?

What would your hug feel like
If you had grown your arms
Enough to wrap around us
The way we would with you?

One Day

I know one day you'll be gone
And I will be here,
Remembering you.

And I'll tell others that you always,
Always remembered
My favorite breakfast.

Every time we enjoyed your meals
You were proud to say
The secret ingredient was, "Amor."

You would roll your eyes at others
And let me be the one to see
So we could laugh in private.

Except I won't see your face again
Outside of pictures
Or my memories.

And I will cry for you
When I am alone in my bedroom
And everyone is asleep.

I'll remember the sound of you

Singing nursery rhymes in Spanish
With me on your lap.

And I'll say to the empty air
Surrounding me,
"Te quiero mucho, Abuelita."

Cuando Se Oye El Grito

Cuando se oye el grito,
I am surrounded by family
And cumbias are playing
While people are dancing.

Cuando se oye el grito,
I am reminded of my culture
And the pride that comes
From making noise together.

Cuando se oye el grito,
I smile because I know
People are having a good time
And I get to be there.

Cuando se oye el grito,
I laugh
And add to the volume
Because I am happy too.

Sí Se Puede

My grandparents are immigrants.
I don't know how hard it was
Aside from my one grandmother's account.
I certainly have not struggled
To the same extent.
She did everything alone,
Using the bus to get around,
Learning as she went,
While having young children to look after.

She came from poverty,
Always sacrificing,
Helping care for her family.
Enduring things from people
Who should have loved her
Because she had no other choice.
Yet I have always known I would have a next meal,
That I would have my own bed to sleep in,
That I could have privacy,
That I would receive gifts on birthdays,
That I could enjoy my childhood,
That I could get a higher education,
That I could want things.

Isn't it strange how suffering and hardship
Can produce some of the sweetest people?
How can there not be found
A single bitter drop in her kind face?
If I had power to shield her from any other harm,
I would in a heartbeat.
I think the only thanks I can give
For inheriting this great love of hers
And that I have opportunities she did not,
Is to see how far I can go
While she proudly watches on.
And I will keep going after,
Because I can't let her efforts be
Wasted with inaction.

Your Words

Your words are very sweet.
I'm not sure you realize
How effective they are on me.

I can tell that my potential
Is an exciting idea to someone like you,
And you see what I can be.

I want you to know that praise
Is water for the roots of love growing in my
heart.
You feed my motivation so effortlessly.

Yet I never give you the proper response
That one might expect because
I'm afraid I'll blush.

Mannerisms

I can see myself in your mannerisms
Which I used to think were only mine.
How could it be that
We are so alike?

Showing instead of saying,
And a little nervous in front of a camera,
Refusing to show our teeth
When smiling in pictures.

Aren't we weird to others
When we just stand there while they talk?
Would our awkward behavior
Like the company of the other?

The Happily Ever Afters

Can a love like the ones we read about really
happen?
My head is full of them,
And I keep placing you and me in the happily
ever afters.

Surely, they were inspired by something real at
some point, right?
Could we have that for ourselves?
Would you be willing to love deeply with me?

You Saw

You saw in me
What I refused to accept
Because I found comfort
In belittling myself.

But you didn't let me
Continue acting as if
My efforts
Were for nothing.
I couldn't avoid addressing
My own negative self-talk
When your own positivity
Shone so brightly on my face.

You said the words so often
That I had to start believing
You must be telling the truth
About me to me.

That my mind is unique,
And I have thoughts to share
With others who will listen.
And I will share them in such a way
That it puts others to shame,
Not because I'm trying to,

But because I simply can't help
But to impress,
And I don't need to apologize
For being great.

Branches

Our roots started far from the other,
And our seeds came from even further.
Yet when the wind blows
And our branches sway,
I feel the edge of my leaves touch yours
And recognize a kindred spirit.
The dew that is on you
Passes onto me
And I can only feel
As though you were made for me
When I feel that I can keep going,
However weak I just was.
Still, our branches touch
As we grow towards the other,
Trying to connect with
That other spirit that
Knows the language we speak
And wants to have
The best conversation
With the other.

Found You

I didn't know someone
Like you could exist
At the same time I do.
Nevertheless, here you are,
And here I am.

I have this feeling,
And that's why
Your presence matters to me.
Because I am painfully aware
Of you when we're in
The same room.
And I can see you
Painfully aware of me too.
So when our eyes meet
We can't help but smile,
Because it feels like
We've been found out
By the other.
We try to find
Something to talk about
Without being obvious.
But we can both feel it.
We're not fooling anybody.